THE Love STORIES OF THE BIBLE Speak

WORKBOOK

13 Biblical Lessons on Romance, Friendship, and Faith

SHANNON BREAM

HarperChristian Resources

The Love Stories of the Bible Speak Workbook

© 2023 by Fox News Network LLC

Requests for information should be addressed to:

HarperChristian Resources, 3900 Sparks Dr. SE, Grand Rapids, Michigan 49546

ISBN 978-0-310-17030-3 (softcover)

ISBN 978-0-310-17031-0 (ebook)

All Scripture quotations are taken from the Holy Bible, New International Version®, NIV®. Copyright © 1973, 1978, 1984, 2011 by Biblica, Inc.® Used by permission of Zondervan. All rights reserved worldwide. www.Zondervan.com. The "NIV" and "New International Version" are trademarks registered in the United States Patent and Trademark Office by Biblica, Inc.®

HarperChristian Resources titles may be purchased in bulk for church, business, fundraising, or ministry use. For information, please e-mail ResourceSpecialist@ChurchSource.com.

First Printing March 2023 / Printed in the United States of America

23 24 25 26 27 LBC 5 4 3 2 1

Contents

Welcome

Love emanates from the heart of God, so we should not be surprised that it's central to the Bible. Throughout its pages, we find the breadth of love expressed in the forms of friendship, family, romance, marriage, and more. But the most foundational type of love is God's unconditional love for His people.

In the upcoming pages, we'll discover a rich tapestry of affection found in 13 love stories from the Bible. We'll explore the first love between Adam and Eve, the surprising love between Ruth and Boaz, as well as the bonding love of Joseph and Mary. Yet love isn't just romantic. One of the most joyous expressions of adoration is found in deep, meaningful friendships like that found between David and Jonathan.

Each loving relationship we'll look at faced similar challenges to the ones we face today. Many faced conflicts and unspeakable challenges. Yet together they remind us that we are designed to both know and to be known. And our relationships are worth fighting for.

May God renew your love for others and Himself as we make this journey together.

* * *

How to Use
This Workbook

This workbook is a companion to the *New York Times* bestselling book, *The Love Stories of the Bible Speak* by Shannon Bream, and it's designed to make your experience richer and deeper. In the upcoming 13 lessons, you'll be challenged to consider the parallels between each love story and your own. You'll be asked to reflect on how God worked in their lives and how He's working in your own.

If you join with friends or neighbors to complete this workbook, consider answering the questions personally *before* you meet up. That way you'll be the most prepared with insights, reflections, and thoughts to share.

You'll notice that each lesson has four components:

*R*EFLECT invites you to read key moments of each person's life in the Bible and connect with their story.

*C*ONNECT asks you to consider how God in the Old Testament or Jesus in the New Testament responds to each person and what this discloses about His character and how He responds to you.

*R*EVEAL provides an opportunity to identify specific character traits, responses to God, and acts of faith, as well as your similar traits, responses, and acts of faith.

*P*RAY asks you to prayerfully consider how the person's story ties into the work God is doing in your life right now.

SONG OF SOLOMON:
The Gift of Love

The principles woven throughout Song of Songs stand in such stark contrast to much of what modern society tells us about relationships. It shows us the truth about God's design for romance, love, and sex. He designed it all! We're given an insider's view into a couple longing to be together but committed to the virtue of waiting to awaken love at its proper time.

—**From** *The Love Stories of the Bible Speak*

*I*n reflecting on love stories of the Bible, it's tempting to think that we'll find a single approach to love. Yet what we discover is love expressed in a myriad of ways including words and actions and tenderness and time and longing and passion.

Song of Songs, also known as Song of Solomon, ranks among the most romantic book of the Bible. This literal love story is chock-full of practical ways to cherish our relationships. While the book doesn't mention God by name, much like the book of Esther, it still contains His truth and presence. Some scholars believe the Song of Songs points to a broader allegory of God's love for Israel and the church. No matter how you read or interpret the book, you'll find marriage as a gift handcrafted by God.

ℛEFLECT

The Lord appeared to Solomon in a dream and said, "Ask for whatever you want me to give you" (1 Kings 3:5). Solomon might have requested celebrity fame or unmeasurable riches or supreme power, but he asked for something striking that pleased the Lord.

Read 1 Kings 3:6–15. What did Solomon ask of the Lord and how did the Lord respond?

Solomon is credited for penning more than 1,000 songs, but Song of Songs is considered his greatest hit. Solomon isn't just the author of Song of Songs, he's also the bridegroom in this beautiful ballad. He's head over heels in love with a Shulamite woman, and language between them is so colorful, some scholars suggested those who struggle with lust should avoid studying it.

Read Song of Songs 1:2–4. How are the woman's senses overwhelmed by the man?

How does the woman specifically express her adoration and love?

Read Song of Songs 1:5–7. How does the woman describe her own appearance?

Read Song of Songs 1:9–11, 15. How does the man respond to the woman?

The man and woman trade heartfelt compliments back and forth. Reflecting on the exchange, how would you describe the intensity of passion and love between the two?

Describe a time when you've felt intense passion and love toward someone.

What did you discover about yourself through that experience?

In Song of Songs 2:1, the bride calls herself, "a rose of Sharon, a lily of the valleys." This flower was lovely and abundant in the region. Rather than a boastful statement, it's an acknowledgement of how she now sees herself because of the bridegroom's love.

Read Song of Songs 2:2. How does the bridegroom describe the woman as exceptional?

What's one compliment you've received that changed the way you saw yourself?

How has being loved by someone transformed you?

How has being loved by God transformed you?

Read Songs 2:7. What does the woman advise and what wisdom do you find in her words?

Though the couple intensely long for each other, they are not blinded by what could steal their joy.

Read Songs 2:15. What are some of the "little foxes" that can ruin the fruit of a beautiful relationship for you? Circle any that you've experienced.

Not prioritizing each other

Allowing criticism to slip in

Underappreciating one another

Small resentments stacking up

Overly busy schedule

An emotional affair
with someone else

Poor boundaries

Making a career top
priority above all else

Keeping secrets

Addiction to shopping, gambling, porn

Undermining each other
in front of the kids

Jealousy toward a partner

Refusing counseling or
professional help

What are three steps you can take to eradicate "little foxes" from your marriage and closest relationships?

❖ _____

❖ _____

❖ _____

Read Song of Songs 2:16. When you think about your relationships, how secure do you feel in being loved?

When you think about your relationship with God, how secure do you feel in being loved by Him?

In chapter 5 of Song of Songs, we once again see the bride yearning for her groom.

Read Songs 5:10–16. What pattern do you notice in the way the bridegroom is described?

> To sit and look at our spouses—really look at them—and to notice all the little things that maybe we have stopped paying attention to, is an act of deep love and selflessness. It's an act that says, "I cherish this person from head to toe."

If you're married, what can you do this week to cherish your spouse from head to toe?

What does Song of Songs reveal about the importance of lavishing praise and adoration on your spouse and those you love?

What does Song of Songs reveal about the importance of complimenting those you love in front of other people?

On the continuum below, mark how easy or hard it is for you to speak words of affirmation to others.

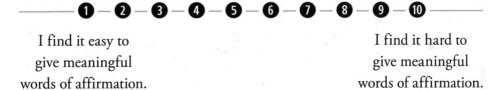

I find it easy to
give meaningful
words of affirmation.

I find it hard to
give meaningful
words of affirmation.

On the continuum below, mark how easy or hard it is for you to receive words of affirmation from others.

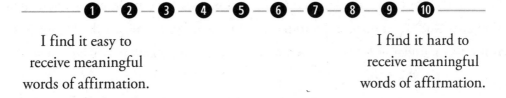

I find it easy to
receive meaningful
words of affirmation.

I find it hard to
receive meaningful
words of affirmation.

Take a moment to think about the words that you speak each day. In your relationships, what best describes the way you respond to others? Circle all that apply.

Loving	Realistic	Kind	Critical
Questioning	Gracious	Cynical	Patient
Know-it-all	Forgiving	Need to be right	Thankful

What changes do you need to make in your words to bring out the best in others?

Read Song of Songs 7:1–13. How do the bridegroom and bride express their desire to be together?

What does this passage reveal about what God desires between a husband and wife?

The poetic language, beautiful and oblique, teaches us to approach sexuality with wonder and care instead of vulgarity or fear. If you're fanning yourself while reading this amorous back-and-forth, remember that God created all of this. He could have simply made us machines for reproduction. But unlike nearly every other type of being to ever exist, God set humans apart to have real pleasure in our physical relationships—within the boundaries he created. Again, not because He wants to make our lives boring—quite the opposite.

His gift to us is the beauty and intimacy of truly connecting with someone we've pledged our lives to and who has given us the same in return. It's in the midst of that security and commitment that we can fully enjoy everything God intended for us. And if we've gotten that wrong at any point, God is a forgiving Father ready to help us work toward His ideal for how we relate to one another.

How has the culture or worldly teaching about sexuality distorted your understanding of what God intends?

In the space below, write a prayer asking God to reveal His truth and remove any distorted teaching from your life.

In the final chapter of this love song, the bride sings of the virtues of love.

Read Song of Songs 8:6–7. What stands out to you about the way the bride describes love?

This bride and groom remind us just how powerful and precious love and the hope for a lifetime bond can be. We should cherish the gift of romance and marriage, nurture and feed it. As our relationships mature, we shouldn't put them on autopilot. Maybe we aren't as gifted as the writer of the Song of Songs, but it doesn't take long to tuck a quick note of appreciation and affirmation into the hands of those we love.

What does it look like to fight for unity and intimacy in your marriage and relationships? Write your response in the space below.

CONNECT

Now that you've read and reflected on much of Song of Songs and the longing between the bridegroom and bride, it's time to connect this love story of the Bible with your own life. Fill out the chart below:

What does this love story teach you about the way you communicate your love to others?	
What stood out to you most in this love story?	
What challenged you most in this love story?	
How do you hope to be more like the bridegroom and bride in the way you express and demonstrate love?	

REVEAL

Now that you've connected this love story of the Bible with your own life, it's time to look at how God reveals Himself and His love through this story to you.

How does this love story challenge you to change the way you love others?	
What does God reveal about Himself, His character, and His desire for loving relationships through this story?	
What does this story suggest or reveal about the way God loves you?	

$\mathcal{P}$RAY

Take a few minutes to ask the Holy Spirit to guide you as you respond to the following prayer prompts:

Lord, like the lovebirds in Song of Songs, help me . . .

_____

_____

_____

_____

_____

Lord, what "little foxes" have I allowed in my loving relationship? What do I need to do to get rid of them?

_____

_____

_____

_____

_____

Lord, where do I most need to grow in expressing and receiving love?

_____

_____

_____

_____

_____

_____

Lord, considering the Song of Songs story, how are You calling me to live differently?

_____

_____

_____

_____

_____

_____

SAMSON AND DELILAH:
MERCY AND RESTORATION

The story of Samson and Delilah has inspired works of art, operas, and movies. It's easily one of the most well-known stories of the Old Testament, yet this couple is a case study into how to get nearly everything about romance wrong. But as with every ancient biblical story of woe, this one is chock-full of lessons for us today.

—From *The Love Stories of the Bible Speak*

*L*et's face it: in the ancient world, as in modern times, sometimes romances are rocky and ultimately destructive. It's impossible to look at love stories of the Bible without looking at one of the most unhealthy and dysfunctional ones of all: Samson and Delilah.

ℛEFLECT

Like Mary, the mother of Jesus, Samson's mother received a heavenly visit.

Read Judges 13:3–5. What special instructions did the angel give to Samson's mother, who was identified as Manoah's wife?

Samson was born into a home where trust and respect resided between his parents. Manoah and his wife were devoted to God's will and to each other. This would prove to be a sharp contrast to the relationships Samson would pursue in adulthood.

Read Judges 14:1–4. Why were Samson's parents hesitant to fulfill their son's blunt request?

Read Exodus 34:16 and Deuteronomy 7:3–4. According to these passages, why was Samson not permitted by the law to marry a Philistine woman?

What does Judges 14:4 reveal about God working through Samson's desire?

The family traveled down to see about this Philistine woman, and along the way, Samson encountered a lion.

Read Judges 14:5–9, Leviticus 5:2–3, and 11:27. Why did Samson avoid telling his parents about the source of the honey?

What do Samson's actions reveal about the compromises he was making as a Nazirite?

Samson appears to be the only "lifelong" Nazirite we meet in Scripture. Generally, the vow was taken for a short period of time. A Nazirite vow didn't just mean no haircuts. God also required Nazirites to not consume wine or strong drink—or even grape juice or grapes! A Nazirite also could never touch a dead body (Numbers 6:1–21).

Where are you most tempted to think you know better than God?

Read Judges 14:12–20. What does this passage reveal about Samson and his wife's character?

⚘ Samson's character:

⚘ Samson's Philistine wife's character:

Read Judges 15:1–8. How did Samson's short-lived marriage end?

Before Samson met Delilah, he had accumulated a lot of baggage. He was shaped by the grief of his first wife, her violent death, and the betrayal of the relationship. He tended to be impulsive and angry, prone to self-destructive theatrics and immature moods. And he was quick to dismiss wisdom.

What are three pieces of baggage that you've carried into your relationships and how are you handling them? Fill in the chart below.

Hurts and Hang Ups: Baggage from the Past	How You've Healed	How You Still Need to Heal

Write a prayer in the space below asking God to complete His full healing work in you.

_____

_____

_____

_____

_____

_____

_____

_____

The Bible tells us that Samson eventually "fell in love" with Delilah (Judges 16:4). This is the first time "love" is used to describe one of Samson's relationships.

Read Judges 16:4–22 and fill in the chart below. Take note of Samson's response to each of Delilah's requests to know the source of his strength.

Scripture	Delilah's Request	Samson's Response
Judges 16:6–9		
Judges 16:10–12		
Judges 16:13–14		
Judges 16:15–22		

Reflecting on the chart on the previous page, how did Delilah's demand of Samson's secret intensify each time she asked?

> Delilah stood to reap more than 82 pounds of silver—an unimaginable sum of money for anyone in the ancient world—much less a woman. That's lottery-jackpot money, the kind of money that would change everything, money that ensured a life of luxury usually available only to kings and queens. Scripture tells us about her motivation in black and white: she did it for money.

Considering Samson's character and past, why do you think he refused to leave the relationship or stop answering Delilah?

Have you ever been in an abusive or toxic relationship that you've been unable or unwilling to leave? If so, describe.

What role did God play in helping set you free?

Read Judges 16:23–31. How did Samson outsmart the Philistines?

How did God redeem Samson and what hope does that give you for God redeeming those you love?

God was still able to use Samson for His purposes. He served as a judge over Israel for 20 years and brutally punished their oppressors, the Philistines.

How much more do you think God could have accomplished through a person who was fully obedient, humble, and honorable?

In the space below, write a prayer asking God to make you obedient, humble, and honorable for His glory.

_____

_____

_____

_____

CONNECT

Now that you've read and reflected on Samson and Delilah, it's time to connect this cautionary love story of the Bible with your own life. Fill out the chart below:

What does this love story reveal to you about unhealthy relationships?	
What stood out to you most in this cautionary love story?	
What challenged you most in this cautionary love story?	
What changes do you need to make to nurture healthy, life-giving relationships?	

REVEAL

Now that you've connected this love story of the Bible with your own life, it's time to look at how God reveals Himself and His love to you through this story.

How does this cautionary love story challenge you to change the way you love others?	
What does God reveal about Himself, His character, and His desire for loving relationships through this story?	
What does this story suggest or reveal about the way God loves you?	

$\mathscr{P}$RAY

Take a few minutes to ask the Holy Spirit to guide you as you respond to the following prayer prompts:

Lord, like Samson's parents, Manoah and his wife, help me . . .

_____

_____

_____

_____

_____

Lord, what baggage am I still carrying in my present loving relationship? How do I begin to heal and be set free?

_____

_____

_____

_____

_____

Lord, where do I most need to draw healthy boundaries and make good decisions?

_____

_____

_____

_____

_____

Lord, considering the story of Samson and Delilah, how are You calling me to live differently?

_____

_____

_____

_____

_____

ADAM AND EVE:

THE ORIGINAL LOVE STORY

A dam and Eve provide us so many rich truths about how God designed a perfect world for humanity, with thoughtful details and beautiful wonders. Adam and Eve also show us what happens when our pride drives us to believe we could be equal to God, chasing our own kingdom instead of pursing and furthering His.

—**From** *The Love Stories of the Bible Speak*

The opening pages of Genesis display a man and a woman building a life together, partnering together as the beginning of all that comes after. There would be no Noah, David, Jonah or Jesus if Adam and Eve hadn't found their way through devastating circumstances in order to stick together and launch the rest of humankind. God launches the whole story of salvation, of humanity's journey to God, with a marriage. Through their love story, we discover God's love story for us.

REFLECT

The creation story unfolds with wonder upon wonder. God hangs the sun and stars in the sky, shapes plants and animals, and eventually handcrafts humankind. God echoes that what He's made is good, until He creates humans, and declares it "very good" (Genesis 1:31).

Read Genesis 1:26–28. What does making humans in His image reveal about how much God loves us?

The second chapter of Genesis provides more details on how God first created humankind.

Read Genesis 2:7. What does God using His breath to give life reveal about His desire for an intimate relationship with us?

Read Genesis 2:18–23. What does this reveal about how God wired you for relationship (romantic, friendship, companionship, etc.)?

On the continuum below, mark how much you wrestle with loneliness.

| I don't wrestle with | I wrestle with |
| loneliness at all. | loneliness all the time. |

Which people has God provided for you to be in meaningful relationship with?

God uses the very same word for Eve that He uses to describe Himself. The word for "helper" in Hebrew is *ezer*. In almost every instance when the word *ezer* is used in the Bible, it is used to describe the saving action of God Himself. God intended for the relationship between Adam and Eve to be one in which they could rely on each other in the same way they relied on God.

Read Genesis 2:16–17 and 3:1–5. How did the serpent twist and sow doubt into what God commanded?

How did Eve substitute her own reasoning for God's?

Read Genesis 3:6–13. What role does blame play in Adam and Eve's response to God?

On the continuum below, mark how much blame slips into your relationships.

I take full responsibility
and never blame anyone for
anything that goes wrong.

I often find others
to take the blame for
anything that goes wrong.

Read Genesis 3:14–19. How did Adam and Eve's idyllic lives change as a consequence to disobeying God?

Once Adam and Eve had acquired the knowledge of good and evil, God noted they couldn't stay in the garden and eat from the Tree of Life. Once removed from the garden, Eve became pregnant with twins and gave birth to Cain and Abel. They soon faced heartache as parents when Cain killed Abel. Yet despite so much pain, they continued to grow together.

Read Genesis 3:20. What did Adam do for his wife?

How did this give Eve a purpose and future?

Where do you most need to be assured God has a purpose and future for you?

> Twice in their lives, Adam and Eve faced unthinkable sorrow. Twice, they reached for each other in response to that sorrow. What we see in the lives of Adam and Eve is a pattern of togetherness and of rebuilding after terrible events that threatened to pull them apart and destroy them.

God ultimately loved all of us so much that He created a way for us to journey back to Him, to spend eternity with Him, rather than separated forever. Through Eve's off-spring, generations later, a child would be born in Bethlehem. Jesus, the Son of God, would offer His life as a sacrifice to bring the long-awaited salvation to the world.

In the space below, write a prayer asking God to grow deeper relationships in which you know and are truly known.

CONNECT

Now that you've read and reflected on much of Adam and Eve and the original love story, it's time to connect this love story of the Bible with your own life. Fill out the chart below:

What does this love story teach you about your own relationships?	
What stood out to you most in this love story?	
What challenged you most in this love story?	
How do you hope to be more like Adam and Eve in the way you face hardship and loss?	

REVEAL

Now that you've connected this love story of the Bible with your own life, it's time to look at how God reveals Himself and His love through this story to you.

How does this love story challenge you to change the way you love others?	
What does God reveal about Himself, His character, and His desire for loving relationships through this story?	
What does this story suggest or reveal about the way God loves you?	

$\mathcal{P}$RAY

Take a few minutes to ask the Holy Spirit to guide you as you respond to the following prayer prompts:

Lord, like Adam and Eve, help me . . .

_____

_____

_____

_____

_____

Lord, where have I become distracted from Your truth, Your ways, and the life You intend? What do I need to do to return wholly and fully to You?

_____

_____

_____

_____

_____

Lord, where do I most need to grow in vulnerability and intimacy with others?

_____

_____

_____

_____

_____

Lord, considering the story of Adam and Eve, how are You calling me to live differently?

_____

_____

_____

_____

_____

JOSEPH AND MARY:
A Bond of Trust

*J*oseph and Mary were thrust into a shockingly unexpected journey, and one that would have been much rockier if they hadn't been unified in their faith and trust of each other—and in God's ultimate plan.

—**From** *The Love Stories of the Bible Speak*

Unlike many of the other relationships described in the Bible, not a single negative word is spoken about Mary and Joseph's marriage. These are honorable people who love God and want to obey Him above all else. Though they face remarkably difficult situations and circumstances, they form a bond of trust with each other and with God. Through their example, we discover the power of sacrifice and selflessness.

REFLECT

The Bible doesn't tell us much about Joseph's background or upbringing, but it does highlight one crucial characteristic: He was a righteous man. Yet living an honorable life doesn't always result in an easy life. Joseph finds himself in a challenging predicament.

Read Matthew 1:18–19. How did Joseph respond to his situation with dignity and compassion toward Mary?

If you thought you had been betrayed in this way, how would you have responded?

Would you have the strength to act with such dignity? Why or why not?

Read Matthew 1:20–24. How did God interrupt Joseph's plans?

How do you respond when God interrupts your plans?

Where are you holding so tightly to what you think your marriage or relationships should look like that you're missing out on what God intends for you?

The angel of the Lord instructed Joseph to name their child Jesus. We must remember that what was happening to Mary wasn't just happening to her alone. It was happening to Joseph, too.

Describe a relationship where something happened to your spouse or friend, and it deeply impacted you.

How did your relationship strengthen or weaken as a result?

What did you learn about navigating hardship with others well through this experience?

Read Ecclesiastes 4:7–12. Fill in the chart below noting the ways healthy, deep relationships are a source of strength.

Scripture	Ways Deep Relationships Strengthen You
Ecclesiastes 4:9	
Ecclesiastes 4:10	
Ecclesiastes 4:11	
Ecclesiastes 4:12	

Though two are mentioned in this passage, verse 12 refers to a "cord of three strands is not easily broken." Many believe that third strand is representative of Jesus.

What role does Jesus play in your three closest relationships? Fill in the chart below.

Name of Person	Role Jesus Plays in the Relationship
1.	
2.	
3.	

Take a moment to reflect on your relationships. Ask the Holy Spirit to reveal any people—perhaps a spouse or friend—who you're thinking of as part of the problem instead of as a source of strength. Write their names below.

❁ _____

❁ _____

❁ _____

❁ _____

In the space below, write a prayer asking God to help you forgive and to change your heart toward each person.

_____

_____

_____

_____

_____

_____

_____

Read Matthew 2:13–20. Describe a time when you faced great loss, suffering, or upheaval. How did this affect your relationship with your spouse or close friend?

How were you drawn closer together or how did the hardship put a wedge between you? Explain.

We don't have many details from the Bible about what happened to Mary and Joseph as a couple after Jesus grew into adulthood. Joseph may have died before Jesus began His public ministry, because at various points in that ministry, His mother traveled with Him and His disciples.

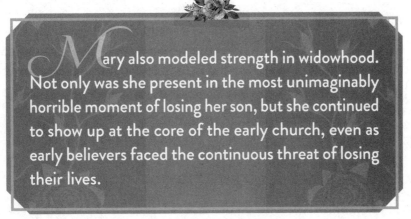

Mary also modeled strength in widowhood. Not only was she present in the most unimaginably horrible moment of losing her son, but she continued to show up at the core of the early church, even as early believers faced the continuous threat of losing their lives.

Read John 19:25–27. What does it reveal about God that Jesus entrusted His mother to His best friend?

In the space below, write a prayer asking God to help you love others well in the midst of hardship and loss.

CONNECT

Now that you've read and reflected on Joseph and Mary, it's time to connect this love story of the Bible with your own life. Fill out the chart below:

What does this love story teach you about sacrificial love?	
What stood out to you most in this love story?	
What challenged you most in this love story?	
How do you hope to be more like Joseph and Mary in the way you express and demonstrate love?	

$\mathcal{R}$EVEAL

Now that you've connected this love story of the Bible with your own life, it's time to look at how God reveals Himself and His love through this story to you.

How does this love story challenge you to change the way you love others?	
What does God reveal about Himself, His character, and His desire for loving relationships through this story?	
What does this story suggest or reveal about the way God loves you?	

$\mathcal{P}$RAY

Take a few minutes to ask the Holy Spirit to guide you as you respond to the following prayer prompts:

Lord, like Mary and Joseph, help me . . .

_____

_____

_____

_____

_____

Lord, in what relationships have I mistaken the problem I'm facing for the person I'm with? How can I make things right?

_____

_____

_____

_____

_____

Lord, where have I fallen into the trap of being right rather than being righteous? How can I demonstrate the fullness of your love and grace?

_____

_____

_____

_____

_____

Lord, considering the story of Joseph and Mary, how are You calling me to live differently?

_____

_____

_____

_____

_____

ESTHER AND XERXES:
Marriage to a Monarch

King Xerxes and Esther's story isn't just a beauty pageant on steroids; it's God's divine work in the midst of a less-than-ideal marriage. Plenty of godly women find themselves in marriages with husbands who don't share their faith. There are plenty of ways to arrive there, but it doesn't mean God can't work through it. It's clear that a faithful woman can change the course of history, whether her spouse is a spiritual leader or not.

—From *The Love Stories of the Bible Speak*

When Xerxes' wife Vashti fails to appear on demand, the enraged king banishes her. Yet God is still working through him. His impetuous response opens the door for the selection of a new queen, and he eventually marries Esther, a faithful and courageous Jewish woman.

Throughout their story, we see Xerxes' growing admiration and eventual joy in granting his wife's deepest wish in her greatest moment of need. These were two imperfect people, but God scripted their story and used what each brought to the table in order to accomplish His divine purposes.

REFLECT

After showboating his wealth and power for 180 days, King Xerxes hosted a party extravaganza for anyone and everyone in Susa. In the Persian court, it was customary for all the subjects to drink when the king took a drink. But Xerxes reversed the custom so anyone could drink anytime without restriction (Esther 1:8). So perhaps we shouldn't be surprised that things soon got out of hand.

Read Esther 1:10–22. How does King Xerxes respond to the Queen Vashti's refusal to appear before him?

What does King Xerxes' response reveal about his character?

What does King Xerxes' response reveal about his view of women and marriage?

Reflecting on the list below, which of the following best describes King Xerxes in this passage? Circle all that apply.

Paranoid	Humble	Distrustful
Open-minded	Angry	Respectful
Power-hungry	Insecure	Wise

During months of beauty preparation, Esther won the favor of all who lay eyes on her (Esther 2:15). But the only one who truly mattered was Xerxes, and he was definitely mesmerized as well. An orphaned Jewish girl soon became the Queen of Persia.

Read Esther 2:15–18. What freedom, decision-making, or choices is Esther given in this passage?

Do you think Esther would have felt more like a prize, a piece of property, or a beloved wife? Explain.

How would you have felt and responded if King Xerxes treated you this way?

As an orphan, Esther had been raised by her cousin Mordecai. He cautioned her not to reveal her Jewish ancestry or family background. With Esther tucked away in the palace, Mordecai stayed as close as possible. One day, while sitting at the king's gate, Mordecai heard two men from the royal court conspiring to kill the king. Mordecai told Esther, who passed the information on to the king and saved his life. This good deed would help Mordecai later on.

With those two men gone, Xerxes elevated his official Haman to the top office. While everyone else groveled at his feet, Mordecai refused to kneel down to him. The infuriated Haman launched a plan to annihilate all the Jewish people—including Mordecai. When Mordecai got word of Haman's murderous plot to Esther, she at first hesitated to go to Xerxes.

Read Esther 4:11. What was at stake if Esther approached the king?

Read Esther 4:12–14. How does Mordecai respond to Esther?

What part of Mordecai's response would have been most motivating for Esther?

Queen Vashti disobeyed a summons and was divorced and banished. Esther risked far more—death—by inventing her own summons.

Read Esther 4:15–17. What does Esther request to help fulfill her dangerous mission?

Read Esther 5:1–5. How does Esther prepare herself to see the king, and how does the king respond?

How would you describe this conversation between this husband and wife?

At the banquet with Haman, the king again reassured Esther that he wanted to grant her deepest wishes, again offering up to half his kingdom.

Read Esther 7:3–10. How does Esther wisely craft her request?

How does the king respond to Esther and Haman?

- ❁ Esther: _____

- ❁ Haman: _____

Read Esther 8:9–11. How did King Xerxes become a defender of the Jewish people?

How do King Xerxes and Esther demonstrate that a relationship—or spouse—doesn't have to be perfect in order for God to work through it?

In the space below, write a prayer asking God to reveal His truth and remove any distorted teaching from your life.

_____

_____

_____

_____

_____

_____

_____

_____

_____

_____

ℭONNECT

Now that you've read and reflected on Esther and Xerxes, it's time to connect this love story of the Bible with your own life. Fill out the chart below:

What does this love story teach you about how people can change?	
What stood out to you most in this love story?	
What challenged you most in this love story?	
How do you hope to be more like Esther in the way you defend, protect, and love others?	

ℛEVEAL

Now that you've connected this love story of the Bible with your own life, it's time to look at how God reveals Himself and His love through this story to you.

How does this love story challenge you to change the way you love others?	
What does God reveal about Himself, His character, and His desire for relationships through this story?	
What does this story suggest or reveal about the way God loves you?	

$\mathcal{P}$RAY

Take a few minutes to ask the Holy Spirit to guide you as you respond to the following prayer prompts:

Lord, like Esther and King Xerxes, help me . . .

Lord, where do I need to be more strategic in the ways I approach and communicate with those I love?

Lord, where do I most need to grow in boldness, courage, and self-sacrifice?

_____

_____

_____

_____

_____

Lord, considering the story of Esther and King Xerxes, how are You calling me to live differently?

_____

_____

_____

_____

_____

RUTH AND BOAZ:
SECOND CHANCES

R uth and Boaz's story didn't start with a love-at-first-sight, thunderbolt-and-lightning kind of moment. It unfolded more slowly. Unlike just about any other love story in the Bible, this was a getting-to-know-you story. These two people were moved by the character and integrity they saw in one another. They each acted in honorable ways. They could have made very different—very selfish—decisions, and yet both Ruth and Boaz put others first and honored their God.

—From *The Love Stories of the Bible Speak*

*R*uth and Boaz weren't a young couple born of an arranged marriage designed to benefit their families. Rather, God is revealed as their ultimate Matchmaker, bringing them together after deep grief and loss. We all know someone who's suffered the loss of a spouse, whether through widowhood or divorce. Maybe you're walking through that challenge right now. That's right where we first meet Ruth.

*R*EFLECT

Sometimes tragedy is made worse by the intensity and frequency of loss. Perhaps this is no truer than in Naomi's family. Naomi lost her husband, Elimelek, but she still had two sons to carry on the family name and watch over her. Each of them married, one to Ruth and the other to Orpah. After about ten years, however, Naomi's two sons passed away as well. In antiquity, that meant these precious women had no one to protect or provide for them.

Read Ruth 1:20–21. What did Naomi begin to believe about God and herself through the tragedies?

Describe a time when you faced a tragedy, anguish, or loss.

What were you tempted to believe about God or yourself that wasn't true?

What role has Scripture played in recentering you on the truth of who God is and what He says about you?

In the midst of her pain, Naomi received the news that conditions in her homeland had improved. She decided to return to Bethlehem. She urged each daughter-in-law to start their lives over with new husbands and families. Orpah fulfilled Naomi's request, but Ruth refused.

Read Ruth 1:16. What did Ruth pledge to Naomi?

What does Ruth's pledge reveal about her faith in God?

When Boaz appears in the story, we quickly learn much about his character and kindness.

Read Ruth 2:1–16. What details about Boaz are revealed in this passage?

How would you describe Boaz in one sentence?

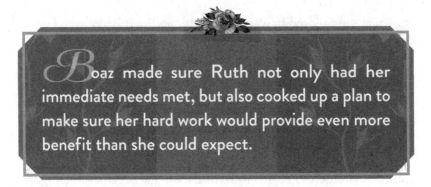

*B*oaz made sure Ruth not only had her immediate needs met, but also cooked up a plan to make sure her hard work would provide even more benefit than she could expect.

Boaz showed compassion to the young widow and outsider working in the fields just to survive.

Who is someone that is suffering you can extend God's love to in practical ways?

Naomi raised the possibility of a match with Boaz and guided Ruth on how to properly approach him in a way in which he might want to take legal responsibility for her.

Read Ruth 3:7–11. How does Boaz' response to Ruth demonstrate respect and dignity?

When it comes to finding love and redemption, Ruth took a huge risk. On the continuum below, mark how easy or hard it is for you to make yourself vulnerable in your relationships.

①—②—③—④—⑤—⑥—⑦—⑧—⑨—⑩

I find it easy to
be vulnerable with others.

I find it hard to
be vulnerable with others.

In the final chapter of Ruth, Boaz acted alone to do what he said he would do. He sat at the gate of Bethlehem where business was often transacted. He approached Naomi's other relative, whose rights to Ruth and the estate were greater than his. The moment the other potential kinsman redeemer realized his property might become entangled with that of Naomi's husband, the man quickly bowed out.

Read Ruth 4:9–10. How does Boaz's response reflect God's love?

How does Ruth's story demonstrate the tender reality and hope of widowed love or of second-chance love?

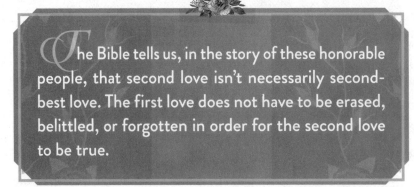

The Bible tells us, in the story of these honorable people, that second love isn't necessarily second-best love. The first love does not have to be erased, belittled, or forgotten in order for the second love to be true.

Read Ruth 4:13–17. How did Ruth's joy spill over to Naomi?

Ruth and Boaz give us a powerful love story that represents God's love for us. Just as Gentiles or non-Jewish people were once outsiders, through Christ they have been gathered to become God's people. Meanwhile, Boaz, the kinsman redeemer, modeled what Christ would do for us. Jesus stepped in with great kindness and compassion to pay the price for each of us. Through His sacrifice, we can have eternal life. Like Boaz, Jesus wraps His acceptance around us and gives us life anew—one full of second chances.

In the space below, write a prayer of thanks for the ways that Jesus has given you forgiveness, shown you kindness, and been your redeemer.

CONNECT

Now that you've read and reflected on Ruth and Boaz, it's time to connect this love story of the Bible with your own life. Fill out the chart below:

What does this love story teach you about second chances?	
What stood out to you most in this love story?	
What challenged you most in this love story?	
How do you hope to be more like Ruth and Boaz in the way you respond to others in need?	

REVEAL

Now that you've connected this love story of the Bible with your own life, it's time to look at how God reveals Himself and His love through this story to you.

How does this love story challenge you to change the way you love others?	
What does God reveal about Himself, His character, and His desire for loving relationships through this story?	
What does this story suggest or reveal about the way God loves you?	

$\mathscr{P}$RAY

Take a few minutes to ask the Holy Spirit to guide you as you respond to the following prayer prompts:

Lord, like Ruth and Boaz, help me . . .

_____

_____

_____

_____

_____

Lord, where have I refused to take the risk of loving others through words and actions?

_____

_____

_____

_____

_____

Lord, where do I most need to grow to show others respect, dignity, and compassion?

_____

_____

_____

_____

_____

_____

Lord, considering the story of Ruth and Boaz, how are You calling me to live differently?

_____

_____

_____

_____

_____

_____

DAVID AND ABIGAIL:
The Rebel and the Peacemaker

Abigail and David's story gives us a look at a difficult marriage, one in which a wife was sent scrambling on a life-saving mission because of her husband's rude arrogance. It's unlikely that Abigail had much choice about her marriage to Nabal, but she didn't wither under his shameful behavior. She was clearly resourceful and trusted by the people of her household. She had found a way to flourish in the midst of a problematic marriage.

—From *The Love Stories of the Bible Speak*

Much of the attention regarding David's marriages circles around Saul's daughter, Michal, as well as his marriage to Bathsheba. Both were marked by seasons of unhappiness and loss. Less attention is given to his relationship with Abigail. The two first crossed paths when David was on the run from King Saul.

ℛEFLECT

A faithful servant to King Saul, David morphed into a threat to the king when his victories as a warrior garnered favor among the people. Saul set out to kill David repeatedly. But when David had an opportunity to kill Saul, he refused.

Read 1 Samuel 24:16–22. How did David demonstrate respect and honor for the man who wanted to murder him?

This story and encounter between Saul and David became the backdrop for David and Abigail's meeting. Whenever someone is first introduced in the Bible, it's important to pay attention to what's said.

Read 1 Samuel 25:2–3. How are Nabal and his wife, Abigail, described?

How would someone describe you and your closest companion?

Read 1 Samuel 25:4–9. How did David demonstrate wisdom and kindness in his approach and request of Nabal?

Read 1 Samuel 25:10–11. How is Nabal's response to David consistent with how he is described in v. 3?

Read 1 Samuel 25:12–13. How does David respond to Nabal?

Read 1 Samuel 25:14–19. How is Abigail's response to David consistent with how she is described in v. 3?

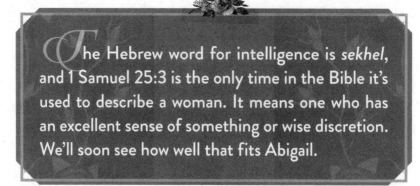

The Hebrew word for intelligence is *sekhel*, and 1 Samuel 25:3 is the only time in the Bible it's used to describe a woman. It means one who has an excellent sense of something or wise discretion. We'll soon see how well that fits Abigail.

Imagine discovering that 400 warriors are headed your way to wipe out your entire household. How would you respond? Circle any that apply.

Panic	Pray	Melt down	Run away
With humility	Hide	Try to intervene	Other: _____

What's one relationship or situation in your life where conflict is escalating?

How are you responding?

Read 1 Samuel 25:23–28. Fill in the chart below noting what roles each of the following played in winning David's favor.

Abigail's Approach	Scripture	How This Helped Win David's Favor
Physical Posture	1 Samuel 25:23–24	
Request for forgiveness	1 Samuel 25:24, 28	
Acknowledgement of wrong or injustice	1 Samuel 25:25	
Words of affirmation	1 Samuel 25:26	
Gifts	1 Samuel 25:27	
Prayer and Faith in God	1 Samuel 25:28–31	
Request for mercy	1 Samuel 25:31	

Consider one relationship in your life where there's conflict or contention. Reflecting on the chart above, how can you pursue peace and restoration with the other person using Abigail's tactics to reach out with humility and grace? Write your answer in the space below.

Read 1 Samuel 25:32–35. What stands out to you most about David's respond to Abigail?

> Just as man sinned against God and created a spiritual crisis, Nabal had offended David, who was looking for payback. Just as Abigail sought to pay the price for her rotten husband, Christ stood in the gap for every human being who would ever need rescue—every one of us!

Read 1 Samuel 25:36–38. How did Abigail continue to demonstrate wise discretion?

Read 1 Samuel 25:39–42. How did David fulfill Abigail's request to remember her?

What do the following passages reveal about handling conflict well? Fill in the chart below.

Bible passage	What it reveals about handling conflict well	Rank in order which you need to grow in the most to the least (1–5)
Proverbs 15:1		
Matthew 5:9		
Matthew 5:24		
Philippians 2:4		
James 1:19		

In the space below, write a prayer asking God to help you become a greater peacemaker and reconciler in all your relationships.

CONNECT

Now that you've read and reflected on the story of David and Abigail, it's time to connect this love story of the Bible with your own life. Fill out the chart below:

What does this love story teach you about how you treat others?	
What stood out to you most in this love story?	
What challenged you most in this love story?	
How do you hope to be more like Abigail?	

REVEAL

Now that you've connected this love story of the Bible with your own life, it's time to look at how God reveals Himself and His love through this story to you.

How does this love story challenge you to change the way you love others?	
What does God reveal about Himself, His character, and His desire for loving relationships through this story?	
What does this story suggest or reveal about the way God loves you?	

$\mathcal{P}$RAY

Take a few minutes to ask the Holy Spirit to guide you as you respond to the following prayer prompts:

Lord, like David and Abigail, help me . . .

_____

_____

_____

_____

_____

Lord, where are you calling me to become an agent of reconciliation?

_____

_____

_____

_____

_____

Lord, where do I most need to grow in grace and humility?

_____

_____

_____

_____

_____

Lord, considering the story of David and Abigail, how are You calling me to live differently?

_____

_____

_____

_____

_____

_____

DAVID AND JONATHAN:
Brothers in Arms

Our Western culture tends to prioritize romantic love above all other kinds of relationships. In the ancient world, friendship was often seen as the most important kind of relationship, and romantic love was a distant second. In David and Jonathan's friendship, we see two people vowing to have each other's backs in very difficult circumstances, not because of obligation—but by choice.

—**From** *The Love Stories of the Bible Speak*

*D*avid and Jonathan grew up in different worlds. Jonathan's father was the king of Israel, and he was raised as a prince. David grew up a pauper taking care of sheep. Despite their different backgrounds, they became the closest of friends. Together, they remind us of the power of the gift of deep friendship.

REFLECT

Under his father's guidance, Jonathan had led men in battle and victory. But the first in-depth introduction to Jonathan comes after Saul failed to follow God's commands and was rejected by Him. While Saul hangs out under a pomegranate tree, reluctant to engage, Jonathan takes his armor-bearer, sneaks into Philistine territory, and springs a surprise attack.

Read 1 Samuel 14:16–23. How does Jonathan demonstrate bravery and dependence on God?

How does this compare to Saul's lack of courage and lack of faith in God?

Like Jonathan, David charged into battle when given the chance to take on Goliath. Like Jonathan, David trusted God to guide and protect him. Following Goliath's defeat, Saul summoned David. Jonathan and David soon became fast friends.

Read 1 Samuel 18:1–4. What does it reveal about Jonathan's character that instead of viewing David as a threat to Saul or himself, he has an immediate kinship?

Describe a friendship in your life that felt instant from the beginning.

Who in your life have you perceived as a threat when you need to see them as a friend?

*B*ecause of Jonathan's friendship with David, David's life would be saved when Saul eventually turned on him. David's survival meant he was able to one day become king of Israel and the ancestor of Christ—meaning one of the reasons you and I are Christians today is the faithful friendship of David and Jonathan.

David's miliary success continued, and Saul's jealousy and contempt exploded as a result. Saul looked not just to marginalize David, but to murder him. That forced Jonathan to pick a side.

Read 1 Samuel 19:1–5. How did Jonathan try to protect and preserve his best friend, David?

Which of your friends have been a powerful advocate for you?

Which of your friends have you protected and advocated for?

Despite Saul's promise that he wouldn't hurt David, he lapsed into madness and rage and tried to spear David. Now, David needed to run for his life. Jonathan struggled to face the hard to truth that his father was trying to murder his best friend. David had to have a difficult but crucial conversation with Jonathan.

Read 1 Samuel 20:1–4. How did Jonathan respond to the unpleasant truth David spoke?

How do you tend to respond when a friend delivers hard or unpleasant truths to you? Place a check mark next to all that apply.

_____ I retreat from the conversation.

_____ I defend myself.

_____ I need time to think.

_____ I look for others to confirm the hard truth.

_____ I look for others to defend me against the hard truth.

_____ I tend to trust my deepest friends and their words.

_____ I respond with grace and humility.

Jonathan and David had an unshakable commitment to their friendship. Jonathan was willing to undermine his own maniacal father in order to save his best friend and honor their pledge of friendship.

Read 1 Samuel 20:16–17. What stands out to you about this beautiful affirmation of friendship?

Who is a friend like Jonathan in your life?

Having communicated using arrows that David was unsafe, the two could have parted without saying goodbye. But David couldn't bear leaving without thanking his closest friend, the person he trusted with his very life. David emerged from his hiding place of safety.

Read 1 Samuel 20:41–42. How do David and Jonathan show appreciation for each other?

When was the last time you told the person you wrote about how much you love and appreciate them?

What's stopping you from expressing gratitude for their role in your life more often?

The Philistines eventually killed Jonathan, and David grieved his death.

Read 2 Samuel 1:25–26. How does David describe his friendship with Jonathan?

We live in a world that is constantly telling us romantic love is the highest ideal, often suggesting that other relationships like friendships are somehow lesser. How does the story of David and Jonathan challenge this kind of thinking?

How does thinking about your friends as gifts from God impact the way you see and treat them?

Who are three of your closest friends? Write a prayer of thanks in the space below for each one.

Name: _____

_____

_____

_____

Name: _____

_____

_____

_____

_____

Name: _____

_____

_____

_____

_____

David and Jonathan provide a rich example of deep, meaningful friendship. But we must remember that God Himself is in a friendship with each of us as believers.

Read John 15:15. What does it mean to you that Jesus calls you His friend?

Where do you most want to grow in friendship with Jesus?

In the space below, write a prayer asking God to deepen your friendship with Him.

_____

_____

_____

_____

_____

_____

_____

_____

CONNECT

Now that you've read and reflected on the friendship of David and Jonathan, it's time to connect this story of the Bible with your own life. Fill out the chart below:

What does this friendship teach you about your friendships with others?	
What stood out to you most in this friendship story?	
What challenged you most in this friendship story?	
How do you hope to be more like Jonathan and David in the way you express and demonstrate love?	

REVEAL

Now that you've connected this story of the Bible with your own life, it's time to look at how God reveals Himself and His love through this story to you.

How does this story challenge you to change the way you befriend and grow in friendship with others?	
What does God reveal about Himself, His character, and His desire for friendship with you through this story?	
What does this story suggest or reveal about the way God desires a relationship with you?	

$\mathcal{P}$RAY

Take a few minutes to ask the Holy Spirit to guide you as you respond to the following prayer prompts:

Lord, like David and Jonathan, help me . . .

_____

_____

_____

_____

_____

Lord, what friendships have I let fade that You're calling me to nurture and reinvest in?

_____

_____

_____

_____

_____

Lord, where do I most need to grow in expressing and receiving love with my friends?

_____

_____

_____

_____

_____

Lord, considering the story of David and Jonathan, how are You calling me to live differently?

_____

_____

_____

_____

_____

SHADRACH, MESHACH, AND ABEDNEGO:
*F*RIENDSHIP IN THE *F*IRE

*I*n the book of Daniel, we meet a group of friends thrown into a terrifying situation that would test everything about their lives and their faith. Stripped away from their families and their homes, the men had God and each other. What a gift God gives us when He blesses us with courageous brothers and sisters committed to standing in unity when trials come.

—**From** *The Love Stories of the Bible Speak*

King Nebuchadnezzar of Babylon laid siege to Jerusalem. Part of the king's plan to subjugate the people of Israel was to keep them from teaching Jewish language, culture, and religion. Everything that made them distinctly Jewish was to be replaced—especially their language, literature, and food. During this period of the Babylonian exile, the Jewish people were forced to find new ways to connect to their faith in a world where there was no more temple, no more land of promise.

REFLECT

King Nebuchadnezzar ordered that Israel's finest men, having been uprooted and carried to a foreign land, be immersed in the Babylonian language and literature.

Read Daniel 1:3–6. How was King Nebuchadnezzar trying to reprogram the Israelites into his culture?

*F*or the Jewish people food was—and is—one of the main ways they obeyed God's commands, by following the kosher dietary laws laid down in the book of Leviticus and elsewhere in the Torah. By denying these young men kosher food, the Babylonians were denying them the ability to worship and obey God as He had commanded them.

Read Daniel 1:8–16. How did Daniel stand his ground regarding the diet?

What does it reveal about the depth of friendship of the four men that they all refused together?

Describe a time when you were in a difficult situation and faith-filled friends stood with you.

How did your friendships grow deeper during that time?

Read Daniel 1:17. How did God bless and provide for this group of friends?

Read Daniel 1:18–20. How did King Nebuchadnezzar show favor to the four friends?

Describe a time when God placed you in a difficult place and gave you the gifts you needed to serve God there.

How did this experience challenge and strengthen your faith?

Afterward, Nebuchadnezzar had a dream. When no one could tell him what he dreamed, he rashly ordered that all the wise men be put to death, including Daniel and his friends.

Read Daniel 2:17–23. How does Daniel rely on his friends during this difficult time?

What role does God and faith play in your closest friendships?

On the continuum below, mark how easy or hard it is for you to ask for prayer from your friends.

①—②—③—④—⑤—⑥—⑦—⑧—⑨—⑩

I find it easy to
ask for prayer
from my friends.

I find it hard to
ask for prayer
from my friends.

What holds you back from asking for prayer from your friends more often?

Who are three friends you can reach out to today and ask for prayer?

❖ _____

❖ _____

❖ _____

Now take a moment and send a text or email asking them for prayer—and offering to pray for them.

Read Daniel 2:46–49. How did King Nebuchadnezzar respond to Daniel's dream interpretation?

Sometime later, King Nebuchadnezzar created a colossal golden idol, ninety feet high and nine feet wide. He demanded everyone bow and worship the image as soon as they heard music playing. The king became furious when he learned that Shadrach, Meshach, and Abednego had refused to obey.

Read Daniel 3:16–18. How were this trio of friends bound together in faith and unwavering commitment to each other?

What challenges and encourages you most about their response to the king?

In a furious rage, the king had the soldiers bind the fully clothed friends and throw them into a furnace heated seven times hotter than usual. The backdraft was so intense, it killed the men who carried out the king's orders.

Read Daniel 3:24–30. How did King Nebuchadnezzar's attitude change toward the following:

Shadrach, Meshach, and Abednego:

The God of Israel:

od not only saved His three faithful servants, but He also showed King Nebuchadnezzar a powerful visual witness to the reality of the true Lord of heaven and earth—the sight of an angel of God. Many scholars believe it was Jesus Himself, protecting and guarding Shadrach, Meshach, and Abednego in the midst of a deadly inferno.

Who is God calling you to rally around when they're facing great challenges?

In the space below, write a prayer asking God to deepen your friendships so that you can stand with others in the fiery trials of life.

CONNECT

Now that you've read and reflected on Daniel, Shadrach, Meshach, and Abednego, it's time to connect these loving friendships of the Bible with your own life. Fill out the chart below:

What do these friendships teach you about the importance of friendship?	
What stood out to you most in these friendships?	
What challenged you most in these friendships?	
How do you hope to be more like Shadrach, Meshach, and Abednego in your friendships?	

REVEAL

Now that you've connected this friendship story of the Bible with your own life, it's time to look at how God reveals Himself and His love through this story to you.

How does this friendship story challenge you to change the way you love and nurture unity among your friends?	
What does God reveal about Himself, His character, and His desire for deep, meaningful, faith-based friendships through this story?	
What does this story suggest or reveal about the way God loves you and desires a friendship with you?	

$\mathcal{P}$RAY

Take a few minutes to ask the Holy Spirit to guide you as you respond to the following prayer prompts:

Lord, like Daniel, Shadrach, Meshach, and Abednego, help me . . .

_____

_____

_____

_____

_____

Lord, where I have avoided stepping into the fire with my friends? How can I become a more loyal, loving, Christ-like friend?

_____

_____

_____

_____

_____

Lord, how are You calling me to be more intentional about talking about faith in my friendships?

_____

_____

_____

_____

_____

Lord, considering the story of Daniel, Shadrach, Meshach, and Abednego, how are You calling me to live differently?

_____

_____

_____

_____

_____

THE FRIENDSHIPS OF PAUL:
Companions for the Journey

I often pictured Paul as a solo traveler, overcoming against all odds, armed with his faith alone, bravely facing beatings, imprisonments, and shipwreck. But the reality is, throughout his ministry, Paul was sustained by friends and companions who made those missionary journeys possible. Each was a joint venture, undertaken by Paul along with at least one other friend.

–From *The Love Stories of the Bible Speak*

*I*n His great love, God knew Paul needed all kinds of friends to carry out the ministry he'd been called to. Paul simply couldn't do it alone. Not only did Paul enjoy trusted colleagues and friends who worked alongside him, he also had multiple churches that supported him through prayer and financial gifts. The birth of Christianity grew through the loving friendships of believers and demonstrates to us how the church grows through the gift of community.

*R*EFLECT

One of Paul's first friendships in ministry was a believer who wasn't interested in having anything to do with him. Paul had a dramatic encounter with God on the road to Damascus during which he was struck blind. In order to have his eyes opened, he needed to go to an unlikely candidate.

Read Acts 9:10–16. What were Ananias' reservations about meeting Paul?

Read Acts 9:17–19. What was the result of Ananias' obedience?

Who in your life did you originally dislike or fear that has now become a trusted friend or encourager?

Paul's encounter with Ananias would be the first of many that would change and support his ministry. One of his most notable friendships was with Barnabas, who became a defender and advocate of Paul (then called Saul).

Read Acts 9:26–28. How did Barnabas build a bridge between the apostles and Paul?

Who is a friend who has advocated or vouched for you among doubters?

Who are three people you can spend your social capital on in order to make sure they get a fair shake?

❀ _____

❀ _____

❀ _____

In the early years of the church, believers were persecuted, and many of them scattered, taking the Gospel with them. When news of the growing church reached the apostles, they sent their trusted friend Barnabas.

Read Acts 11:22–26. How did Barnabas cultivate and honor the talents of Paul in Antioch?

That word "faithful" was at the heart of all Paul's friendships: Christ's love and truth were at the core. The Lord was the common thread in his community, and love of Jesus was what sustained their bonds. Paul shows us that when we share Jesus with someone we love, that bond becomes unbreakable—even in the face of disagreements or catastrophe.

The friendship between Barnabas and Paul was something the Lord wanted to use in powerful ways.

Read Acts 13:1–3. Who is someone God's partnered you with to serve and love others?

How are you nurturing and protecting this friendship?

Together, they faced all kinds of dangers, resistance, and missionary journeys. But like all relationships, they also had disagreements. At one point, they clashed over who should accompany them on a trip. Barnabas wanted to bring his cousin, John Mark, but Paul didn't want to because of a previous experience with him (Acts 15:38).

Read Acts 15:39–40. When have you had such a sharp disagreement that you had to part ways?

Even though they were no longer traveling together, Paul clearly still thought highly of his friend. Paul defended their right to receive financial support from the communities they supported spiritually.

On the continuum below, mark how easy or hard it is for you to disagree with someone yet still honor and respect the person.

① — **②** — **③** — **④** — **⑤** — **⑥** — **⑦** — **⑧** — **⑨** — **⑩**

| I find it easy to disagree and yet still honor and respect the person. | I find it hard to disagree and yet still honor and respect the person. |

What changes do you need to make in your attitudes and actions to honor and respect those you disagree with?

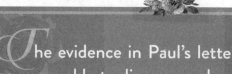

The evidence in Paul's letters tells us that they were able to disagree and move on without nurturing resentment toward each other. In fact, in later years John Mark was mentioned by Paul with approval (Colossians 4:10), suggesting that the friction between them had been put to rest. Paul urged that Mark be welcomed.

Paul developed friendships throughout his many travels, and he celebrates many of them through his letters.

Read Colossians 4:7–15. Who does Paul acknowledge and appreciate in this passage?

What steps do you need to take to develop a wider network of spiritual friends in your life?

In the space below, write a prayer asking God to reveal who He is calling you to reach out to and grow deeper in your relationship with. Record any names that come to mind and reach out to those people this week.

CONNECT

Now that you've read and reflected on the friendships of Paul, it's time to connect this story of the Bible with your own life. Fill out the chart below:

What do the friendships of Paul reveal about the importance of your friendships?	
What stood out to you most about Paul's friendships?	
What challenged you most about Paul's friendships?	
How do you hope to be more like Paul in your friendships?	

REVEAL

Now that you've connected this story of the Bible with your own life, it's time to look at how God reveals Himself and His love through this story to you.

How do Paul's friendships challenge you to change the way you nurture and invest in others?	
What does God reveal about Himself, His character, and His desire for spiritual relationships through Paul's friendships?	
What does this story suggest or reveal about the way God loves you?	

$\mathcal{P}$RAY

Take a few minutes to ask the Holy Spirit to guide you as you respond to the following prayer prompts:

Lord, like Paul and his friends, help me . . .

_____

_____

_____

_____

_____

Lord, where have I pulled back from investing in the friendships You've given me? Which friendships do I need to rekindle?

_____

_____

_____

_____

_____

Lord, where do I most need to grow in showing respect and honor to those I disagree with? What relationships do I need to go back and make right because I handled a disagreement poorly?

_____

_____

_____

_____

_____

Lord, considering Paul's friendships, how are You calling me to live differently?

_____

_____

_____

_____

_____

JOB AND HIS FRIENDS:
COMPANIONS IN GRIEF

*F*riends show up in so many ways in our daily lives, but sometimes it takes a real crisis to see the full blessing of their presence and kind words. They aren't perfect; none of us are. But a true friend's intentions are always pure, even if they fumble in their efforts to comfort us. That's at the heart of the Old Testament story of Job's grief and the friends who showed up in his darkest hour.

—**From** *The Love Stories of the Bible Speak*

*J*ob lost nearly everything. When his friends—Eliphaz, Bildad, and Zophar—showed up, they tried to help Job wrestle with the meaning of what had happened in his life. Not everything they said was true or accurate, but the fact that they showed up and struggled to engage with these problems alongside him makes this book an extended meditation not just on suffering but on friendship.

REFLECT

One of the most meaningful stories in the Bible for those who are suffering is found in the book of Job. The first time we meet this man, we discover his faithfulness to God.

Read Job 1:1–5. How does Job demonstrate his love and respect for God?

Read Job 1:6–12. What is Satan's argument against Job?

Satan's question is an uncomfortable one, and it can—and should—make us dig into our own motivations. Take a moment to honestly answer the following:

- ❀ How do all the blessings God has given you impact your love and respect for God?

- ❀ What would your relationship with God be like if all the blessings were taken away?

Job's losses, including his wealth, children, health, and support of his wife, were unbearable. Yet Job's friends rallied around him.

Read Job 2:11–13. What do Job's friends do well in this passage?

Which of Job's friends' actions can you put into practice?

Job's friends showed up and offered the gifts of presence, shared grief, and silence. So often, when someone we know has suffered a terrible loss, we hesitate to reach out because we feel awkward or worry our words will come out all wrong. Just do it. Looking away from a friend's pain will always be the wrong strategy. Plunge into the anguish with them. Just show up.

Eliphaz was the first of Job's friends to speak to him, and he addressed Job's despair.

Read Job 4:1–9. How does Eliphaz blame Job for the calamity?

Read Job 5:17–18. How does Eliphaz tell Job that this is God's correction?

Describe a time when someone responded to your pain with untruth or misguided advice.

How did you respond?

Eliphaz isn't the only friend who claimed Job's woes were a result of his sin.

Read Job 8:4. What does Bildad blame for Job's loss?

Read Job 11:1–6. How does Zophar respond to Job and his loss?

By steadily resisting their explanations for suffering, Job was challenging more than just his friends' ability to be good comforters. He was questioning everything they thought they knew about God and the universe. He was suggesting that their ideas might be wrong. That's an uncomfortable place to be, so his friends reacted in anger, frustration, and even confusion.

The friends thought they were offering support by helping Job figure out where he had gone wrong; they only ended up causing him more pain.

Why is trying to provide a "why" to people's unspeakable pain so unhelpful?

In response, Job suggested that their view of God might just be too small.

Read Job 12:13–21. In the midst of so much unknowable pain, why is it crucial to remember the mystery of God?

How do you respond when your friends challenge you on spiritual matters?

On the continuum below, mark how you tend to respond to others.

①—②—③—④—⑤—⑥—⑦—⑧—⑨—⑩

I am always listening
to how God may be
speaking through my friends.

I tend to insist
on my views as
the best and most biblical.

Job's friends were way off. They attempted in arrogance and foolishness to reach a conclusion and provide certainty about Job's suffering. God eventually showed up to defend Job and reveal His power and might through creation. And God restored twice as much as he had before (Job 42:10).

Yet God wasn't happy about the way Eliphaz, Bildad, and Zophar had handled themselves.

Read Job 42:7–9. Why was God angry?

What role did Job play in their restoration?

In the space below, write a prayer asking God to help you be a source of healing and true comfort to those who are grieving and walking through hard seasons.

_____

_____

_____

_____

CONNECT

Now that you've read and reflected on Job and his friends, it's time to connect this story of the Bible with your own life. Fill out the chart below:

What does this story teach you about the way you communicate your beliefs to others?	
What stood out to you most in this story?	
What challenged you most in this story?	
How do you hope to be like Job's friends? How do you hope to avoid being like Job's friends?	

REVEAL

Now that you've connected this friendship story of the Bible with your life, it's time to look at how God reveals Himself and His love through this story to you.

How does this story challenge you to change the way you love others in times of grief?	
What does God reveal about Himself, His character, and His desire for loving relationships through this story?	
What does this story suggest or reveal about the way God loves you?	

$\mathscr{P}$RAY

Take a few minutes to ask the Holy Spirit to guide you as you respond to the following prayer prompts:

Lord, like Job's friends, help me . . .

_____

_____

_____

_____

_____

Lord, what have I said to others that was meant to heal but instead caused hurt?

_____

_____

_____

_____

_____

Lord, where do I most need to sit in loving silence with my friends?

_____

_____

_____

_____

_____

Lord, considering Job and his friends, how are You calling me to live differently?

_____

_____

_____

_____

_____

JESUS AND JOHN:
FRIENDS FOR ETERNITY

*F*riendships are part of the human experience. God created us for community, and Jesus was no exception when He walked among us in human flesh. Christ's ministry was spread through strong relationships, forged in both grace and persecution. Jesus built His life around those friendships and left us a model of human love we can apply today.

—From *The Love Stories of the Bible Speak*

*I*n coming to take on a human body and live among us, experiencing all that earthly life entails, Christ showed us how to live while fully embracing both the spiritual and the physical elements of life. Jesus' friendships teach us just as His parables and sermons do. He was God, and He had close friends. In Him we see how seeds of connection, watered with selflessness and intention, can blossom into unbreakable bonds.

ℛEFLECT

John's relationship with Jesus provides encouragement and insights on how to be close to Christ in a spiritual sense and how to walk with Him as a friend. It also demonstrates how much Jesus loves us in our weaknesses and with our unique personalities.

Read Mark 3:13–19. What name does Jesus give to John and his brother James?

Read Mark 9:38–40. How is John overly zealous in this passage?

Read Luke 9:51–55. How is John overly zealous in this passage?

John continues to grow in his deep loyalty to Jesus, and with time, he learns to temper his fiery passion. The first letter of John challenges Christians to abound with love and patience.

Read 1 John 4:7–12. What does this passage reveal about how John and his attitudes were transformed by his relationship with Jesus?

John was part of Jesus' inner circle, which also included Peter and James. These three disciples were given front row seats to some of Jesus' most profound moments and miracles.

Fill in the chart below, noting the special moment the disciples witnessed in each passage and what they discovered about Jesus or their humanity through it.

Scripture	Discovery about Jesus and/or Themselves
Mark 5:35–43	
Matthew 17:1–3	
Matthew 26:36–46	

In the final twenty-four hours of Jesus' life, John was there for Him in a way none of the others were, except for His own mother. When Jesus was arrested, Peter and John followed Him at a safe distance. Only John was "known to the high priest" (John 18:16) and was allowed to follow Jesus into the inner courtyard of the high priest's residence, while Peter had to warm himself at the fire with the servants. This gives John's account an eyewitness quality; it is the testimony of one who was there and saw the worst of Jesus' trial.

John was an eyewitness to the events of the crucifixion and the resurrection.

Read John 20:3–8. What did John see that sparked his belief?

Read John 13:23 and 19:26. What phrase does John use to describe himself?

What does this phrase reveal about where John found his identity?

What does this phrase reveal about what John had discovered about friendship with God?

What holds you back from describing yourself with the same phrase?

Jesus broke down any distance between Himself and His followers. *You're not just someone at arm's length; you are truly My friends.*

Read John 15:12–15. What is the greatest love you can demonstrate with your life?

Prayerfully consider where God is calling you to love greatly right now. Write your response in the space below.

CONNECT

Now that you've read and reflected on the friendship of Jesus and John, it's time to connect this story of the Bible with your own life. Fill out the chart below:

What does this story teach you about friendship with Jesus?	
What stood out to you most in this story?	
What challenged you most in this story?	
How do you hope to be more like John in your friendship with Jesus?	

REVEAL

Now that you've connected this story of the Bible with your own life, it's time to look at how God reveals Himself and His love through this story to you.

How does this love story challenge you to change the way you love God?	
What does Jesus reveal about Himself, His character, and His desire for a relationship with you through this story?	
What does this story suggest or reveal about the way Jesus loves you?	

$\mathscr{P}$RAY

Take a few minutes to ask the Holy Spirit to guide you as you respond to the following prayer prompts:

Lord, like the friendship between You and John, help me . . .

_____

_____

_____

_____

_____

Lord, where am I holding back in truly loving You with everything?

_____

_____

_____

_____

_____

_____

Lord, where do I most need to grow in expressing and receiving love with You?

_____

_____

_____

_____

_____

Lord, considering the friendship between John and You, how are You calling me to live differently?

_____

_____

_____

_____

_____

_____

HOSEA AND GOMER:
God's Unconditional Love for Us

*I*magine having the strength not only to forgive your betrayer, but also to embrace them with love and kindness after their duplicity has been fully exposed. That's what our Heavenly Father does for us day after day, minute after minute, second after second—no matter how many times our faithless hearts wander from Him.

—From *The Love Stories of the Bible Speak*

Only God can provide unconditional love in its purest form. His immovable love for us is beautifully portrayed through one of the Old Testament's most difficult stories: Hosea and Gomer. Through it, we discover the lengths God will go to rescue us and restore us—no matter what.

ℛEFLECT

The prophet Hosea was given an incredibly challenging assignment from God. It's one many of us would have balked at!

Read Hosea 1:2. What difficult assignment did God give Hosea?

How would you respond if given the same assignment?

At the time of Hosea's ministry, the people of Israel were, once again, wildly off course. Under King Jeroboam II they were doing well politically and, from a worldly perspective, prospering. Yet their hearts were chasing after everything but the God who had delivered them out of slavery in Egypt hundreds of years earlier. They were also a divided kingdom, with Israel to the north and Judah to the south. Idolatry and immorality were common practices, as were bribes and corruption.

Read Hosea 1:4–8 and fill in the chart below noting each child of Hosea's name and meaning.

Scripture	Child's Name	Meaning
Hosea 1:4		God scatters
Hosea 1:6		
Hosea 1:9		

How do the children's names represent the breakdown of the Israelites' relationship with God?

Despite what looks like a hopeless situation, God reveals He has a plan and purpose.

Read Hosea 1:10–11. What does God promise to do?

Read Hosea 2:1–8. How does God make the Israelites' lives difficult in order to draw God's people back to Himself?

Read Hosea 2:14–23. What is the purpose of the hardships the Israelites face?

What is God's ultimate promise and plan for His people?

As if Hosea's assignment wasn't already challenging enough, God asks Hosea to do something even more difficult.

Read Hosea 3:1. What does God ask Hosea to do?

How does this command represent God's unfailing love for His people?

> We all want to be Hosea in this story, but we're Gomer. We desire to be the hero, but on a spiritual level we're always going to be the one who needs to be rescued. It's easy to point the finger elsewhere, but what we usually need is a mirror. God's boundless love for us is limitless, meaning He is always pursuing us and calling for us to abandon our selfish wanderings.

Though it's easy to want to be Hosea in this story, it's important for us look at where our responses are more like Gomer. Take a few moments to prayerfully respond to the questions below.

How am I being selfish?

_____

_____

_____

_____

How have I become self-centered?

How am I compromising or cutting corners?

Where am I flaunting my sin?

What am I loving more than God?

What am I worshiping other than God?

_____

_____

_____

_____

God's boundless love is limitless, meaning He is always pursuing us and calling us to abandon any selfish wanderings. God is always beckoning us back to Himself and waiting open-armed to embrace us. In the New Testament, God's love toward us is demonstrated through Jesus Christ.

Read Romans 5:7–8 and 1 John 4:10. What do these passages reveal about the depths of God's love?

Take a moment to reflect that the Creator of this universe lowered Himself to become human and experience every temptation and trial we face, knowing His life on earth would ultimately end with someone close to Him delivering Him into the very hands that would brutally torture and execute Him. Before you ever existed, God loved you that much.

How do you respond to that kind of love?

Not only can we receive this love from God through Christ, but we can become conduits of this love to others. What do the following passages reveal about demonstrating God's unconditional love to others? Fill in the chart below.

Scripture	How to Demonstrate God's Unconditional Love
Matthew 5:43–47	
Matthew 25:35–40	
Romans 15:1	
1 Corinthians 10:24	
Philippians 2:3–4	

Who are three people you know who most need to experience God's unconditional love?

❖ _____

❖ _____

❖ _____

How can you demonstrate that unconditional love to each of them?

❖ _____

❖ _____

❖ _____

In the space below, write a prayer asking God to help you both experience and extend the depths of His unconditional love.

_____

_____

_____

_____

_____

_____

_____

CONNECT

Now that you've read and reflected on God's unconditional love, it's time to connect this love story of the Bible with your own life. Fill out the chart below:

What does this love story teach you about how far God will go to draw you back to Himself?	
What stood out to you most in this story?	
What challenged you most in this story?	
What steps do you need to take to be more faithful to God?	

ℛEVEAL

Now that you've connected this love story of the Bible with your own life, it's time to look at how God reveals Himself and His love through this story to you.

How does this love story challenge you to change the way you love God? Love others?	
What does God reveal about Himself, His character, and His desire for loving relationships through this story?	
What does this story suggest or reveal about the way God loves you?	

$\mathcal{P}$RAY

Take a few minutes to ask the Holy Spirit to guide you as you respond to the following prayer prompts:

Lord, like Hosea, help me . . .

_____

_____

_____

_____

_____

Lord, like Gomer, help me not to . . .

_____

_____

_____

_____

_____

_____

Lord, who are You calling me to share the Good News of Your unconditional love with?

_____

_____

_____

_____

_____

_____

Lord, considering Your unconditional love, how are You calling me to live differently?

_____

_____

_____

_____

_____

_____

ABOUT THE AUTHOR

Shannon Bream is the author of the number one *New York Times* bestsellers *The Women of the Bible Speak* and *The Mothers and Daughters of the Bible Speak*, the anchor of *Fox News Sunday*, and the Fox News Channel's chief legal correspondent. She has covered landmark cases at the Supreme Court and heated political campaigns and policy battles from the White House to Capitol Hill.

ALSO AVAILABLE
FROM SHANNON BREAM

Wherever books are sold.

Chrystal Evans Hurst

Lisa Whittle

Wendy Blight

Sandra Richter

Lysa TerKeurst

Karen Ehman

Lynn Cowell

Jada Edwards

Jennie Allen

Christina Caine

Shannon Bream

Ruth Chou Simons

Ann Voskamp

Sarah Jakes Roberts

Rebekah Lyons

Megan Marshman

Lori Wilhite

Anne Graham Lotz

Lisa Harper

Margaret Feinberg